KING SATURN'S BOOK

Poems by David Annwn

David Annwn

Drawings by Peterjon Skelt

Copyright (c) David Annwn and Peterjon Skelt 1987
Published by North And South at
25 Crockerton Road, Tooting, London SW17 7HE and at
53 Teall Street, Ossett, Wakefield, Yorkshire   WF5 0PA

North and South is a member of the Association of Little Presses (ALP)

Printed and bound by Dawes Press Ltd at
68 Dawes Road, London   SW6 7EJ

ISBN 1 870314 00 X

Published in an edition of 500 of which this is number *238*

For Adele,
who shared the first return

For John and Sonia Skelt

King Saturn's Book

In a society that was switching from an agrarian to an industrial base, the clock and the city are two appropriate symbols of a world whose outermost planet was known to be Saturn.

Daniel Heydon

What survives our history ?
What will time illuminate,
Loosed as glistening Autumn light
Fills our borders, storms your eyes ?

Twisted heaps of fallen leaves,
Blood—red jointures of the stem —
Veinings after confluence,
Catch the shadow, blear the name

II

No outward violence yet enfolds
These solitary terms of cold.
I never expected the ground so cold.
The painted myrtle fears the tense,
Runs its forces swift to ground,
Wipes the air confusedly.

Pigeons mime nativity,
Raise for me their varnished necks,
Gray, embittered purples, browns.
Saturn's little messengers
Down on these diagonals.

III

Though there's nothing simple,
Simply say,
There must be something more,
Than blankness or commodity
Behind the store of your stare

And that we are all sold for,
God in Heaven, every day.

IV

Overnight the snow will come,
Blanks of grayness fill the space
Inhabiting the planet's dream,
In quietness will come the snow,
Falling almost formally,
Ornately—clustered tinges
Adding weight to winters
Already tense inside the stem.

V

A fortunat ascendent – clepen they whan that no wicked planete,
as Saturne, or Mars or elles the Tayl of the Dragoun, is in the
hous of the ascendent.

A Treatise on the Astrolabe

This could be anywhere terrible,
Answer: Why did you bring me here ?
For Pain is its own landscape;
Did you not have a say in the matter,

Before the salt—trailed glacier
Broke your blue eyes' clarity

Once like a pick from the glacial sea
And who is steering this person ?

VI

Is that any way to speak to yourself ?

Giant Saturn is eating his children,
His islanded home, over and over.

VII

The Prophetess of Knaresboro

Mother Shipton knew the score:
The sticklebacked spine of England,
Curled, invested with foundry flares,
Mechanization walking on air.
Moulded into this stretch—marked stone,
Petrified signa : a helmet, a doll,
Stalactite stocking blessed with the pour —
Saw the land heaving in labour,
Terrible conflagration.

VIII

They issue again, they come,
All the imaginary Royalists
Tricked up just as I needed them,
New as a bone unclothed in clay,
Speaking at Tennis, Gustavus Adolphus,
Ready for play on their Deity's fields.

History sits with their crooked grin,
Yields us Naesby : flourishes
Blinkered helmet, keeled cuirass,
Calling to image their slit—nosed whores.

— 'As God is my witness, fire become servitude.'

I   This is how the city begins

IX

And fire tongued armour,
Brazen, almost diffidently.

Bilbrough manor frames the view,
A walker's sight is cut by trees
Then lazes:
>   'Through groves of pikes he thundered then,'
>   'General Fairfax,' praised the pen
>   That winced to draw the hill's soft brow,
>   Smoother than a cow's.
These 'oracles' of oak
Marvell disparages,
Bearing too few garland—crowns
To celebrate 'one fertile year'
His lord spent steepling trenches,

'And mountains raised of dying men,'
Choking on their dialects.

X

Redbank

In blood—starred wars our common weal...

As Cromwell watched them from the farm,
Roundheads set on meet estate
Mobbed the narrows, took the crest,
And cannoneers, their minds repelled
By every lignite hiss and thud,
Rooted men and planted them
Skyward legs in scurried ground —

Sand well—versed in martyrdom,
St. Oswald's offered sanctuary,
Cherished stone and hand—smoothed font;
Some screeched like rats
And slapped into the Mersey.

II   Who is steering this person

XI

Snow is barbarous in its falling,
It comes down stilly, it flurries
Against the pigeon's rest.
Prinked by sparrow's feet
Still it is unsettling, forming
Levels of its unrest.

There was not, nor ever is
Place to regard the eye,
Space to guard the light–opening.
Rooms where mothers and fathers sit
Frame their children's glint
With caring, arbouring fingers.

Snow is unwinding all over the land,
Estates and gardens and engines,
Injurious, cold, its song
Shivered in that chill regard:
O God, the aged,
Breathing in their sleet–blown house.

Radio playing, blurs all day,
Lovers next door think she's gone;
Where is this terrible winding,
Undoing endless patience,
Of heart's clear stem,
Where I have offended, or not

Undoing the grace–knot, the snow ?

III *Levels of unrest*

XII

Bath

O Purcell, you are pert,
Airily so keen,
The underswelling yeomanry
Voice of the British square at Ramille.

Babies are dying from Pulteney Bridge,
Down to the hulks of Oldfield,

Heavily—drugged, long—cartilaged men
Crying, they hobble the perfumed sedan
To broken marl at Crescent—ends;
This is how the city begins.

XIII

Deeper and yet deeper into dream,
yourself in images bent over yourself,
Distorted, only faintly seen.
This really can't be happening,

Freeze that aches to be out of flesh
Drawing you on to bluer ice,
Jagged splinters glint underneath.
Face — a flash—point of daggered fish,
Your glistenings and darknesses.

IV *Who looks through the sea*

XIV

For Alan Richardson

City of oolite geommetries,
Rainworn flowers eating on stone,
I felt like a Celt in the forum:

Enclave of the desiderate hosts,
Bomb—proof curtains in old hotels,
Run—down, recidivist tea—rooms.

On 'Festival Day' Beau Nashe's ghost
Might have flustered — wigged and masked,
Plumed cock struts his brightening cage,

Feathered gilt on railings, mottoes,
'See the flags and trailers furling ...'
O my friend, ahead of us,
Stands, in time, the obdurate time
Settling through our various lives,
Love's resort or ignorance.

XV

Nude

What I would see :
Pale body's extension
Of the poem's loneliness.

V *Point of daggered fish*

XVI

Live where you're paid
Do what you can

Some nights work out so terrible
Nine months without a woman,

No visions, just a motorway
Stretching to the motel's red,

Lights along the shoulder—curve
Glistering signs of failure,

No gods, no goods, no still, small voice
Can keep me through till morning,

No hope of warmth in other lives,
Just booze – my love, my warning.

XVII

Dynasties of corn—fattening gods
Displacing each other,
Toppling like sods down the sides of old middens.

You, as well, an outcast of sky,
Chose to inhabit an Italiante fort,
Vine—rich fissures – territories.

In lore, a scrawny threadbare rex,
In Artifex: 'Constrictor,'
Chief of Malevolent Deities.

VI *Gardens and engines*

XVIII

> 'Iam nova progenes celo demttitur alto,
> Iam rediet virgo, redeunt saturnia regna.'
>
> **The First Shepherd's Play**

To the Makere of Plays

'Good luf and charyte blendyde amanges us.'
The 'Wakefield Master' know his folk,
How to furnish virgin–birth.

Even pagan Virgil's pen
Traced the thread through history —
Sensed a gleam in burdened woods.

Scenes, still held, like photographs:
Snow on gray — or planter's skill
Grafting the vine to whitethorn's ghost,
Haunting the iris afterwards.

> Out of the dark—
> 'new kynde is send
> amiss to mend
>
> with peace and plenty
> Saturn shall bend...'

To the timely and well–heeled
Merchants standing in a ring.

Angels trim the age, set sail:
Ships full of bales, purposive hoards

Into the minds of passionate shepherds.

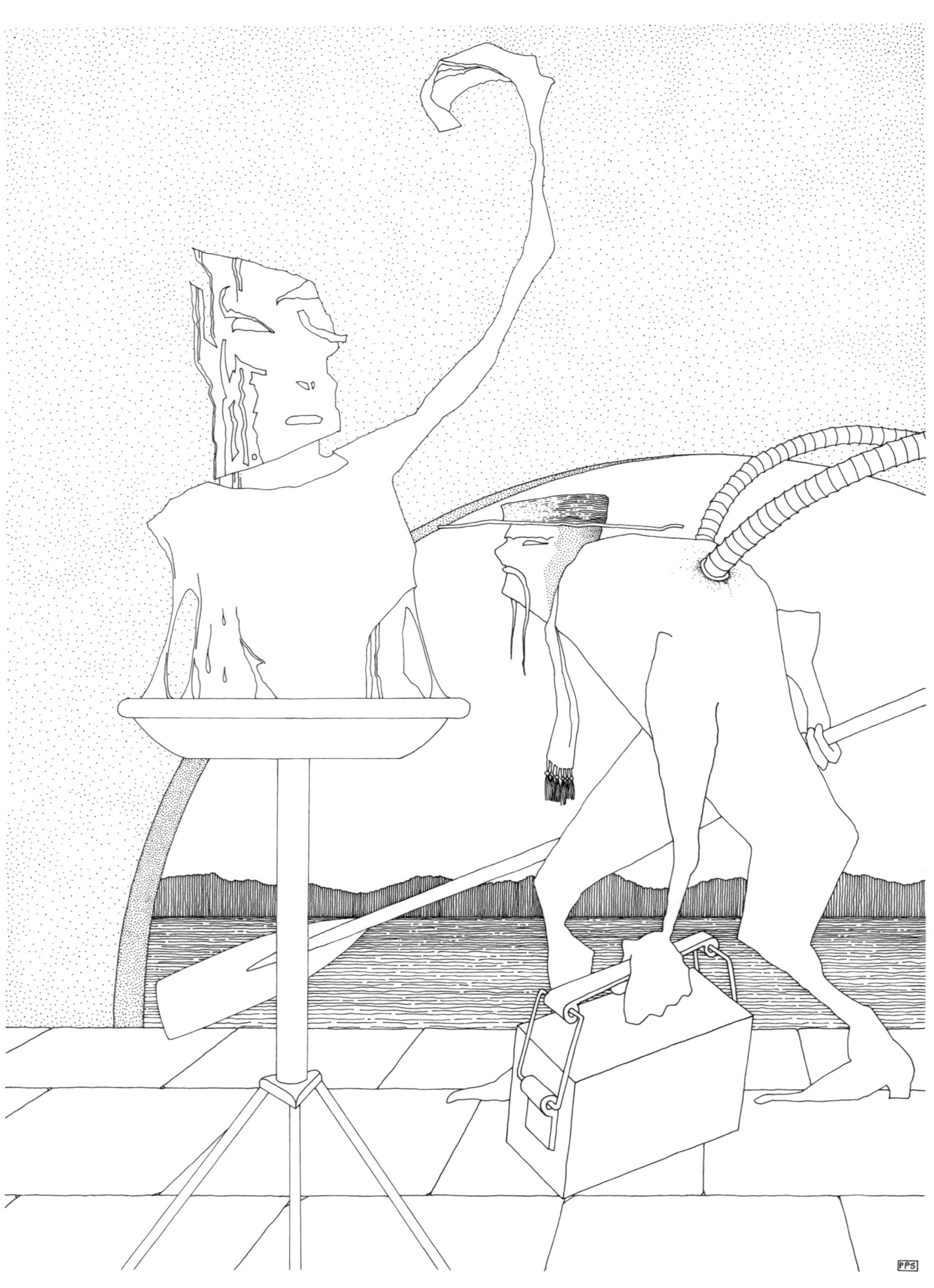

VII Oarsman of the evening

XIX

Speech came then as after long silence,
Staring, hearing the night relapse
Into all—sensing that borders on us:
Coolly the eyes of indifferent pigeons
Seal our mind's unformly wax,
Finely distinguished — the crook and the crux —
Saturn's grim insignia.

VIII *All I have seen will end just like this*

(Corixa Punctata)

The flying boatman is coming,
At Autumn's beginning and garden—end,
Into the pendulous, weeded pools.

The staling smell of winey piss
Drifts from railway—cuttings,
Willow—herb unwreathes its seeds.

In similar air, in self—same air,
While families, televisions,
And sofas pale their obscure rooms,

Comes the dark air's susurrous,
Edging warmth and water,
Thoroughfares of snail and fish.

Its sting — a mouth—sprung, thrashing sting,
Can burst the soft, gold undersides
of quiet—breathing Midases.

Rowing in its painted hull,
Oarsman of the evening,
Solving Summer's muddled dreams,

Clear beneath the Winter's skull.

Extracts from a Journal

1

New worlds of viscosity rise above the fields.
On Budle Shore at Lindisfarne
All I can offer are notes from a journey,
Estuary glints, an unsellable mead,
Concatenations of squalling birds.
While some propound its efficacy:
Aidan and Oswald – unfinished arches,
Breathe in a second from priory swards,
Morticed in sections, tailored in stone.
Their cross is the glans in a jellyfish–bell,
Coptic and swirled. I have gone down,
Crustacean reds, cetacean greens,
Pebbles hard upon my bed;
With de–pincered membra lay a horizon,
Gray like turbulence backing a wave.
These are the season's waft off the sea.

2

This is the Wye, we sit by the river
Reading American poetry.
Sensation offers disorderly blurrings,
Cool and undulant following water,
Mud–red flowing to Herefordshire.
Flow back, flow backwards,
Is there a centre,
Though I am far from the mystical Wye ?

3

At Kilpeck, bridge of dreams and sighs,
Sanctuary bridge of wishes and promises,

Aries and Pisces, Siamese–twinned,
Gargoyled and Norman, subterrene Gemini,

Globing like fruit from sutured stone,
All this becomes you — the colour of dreams,

Cuts on an empire a nation's erosions;
All I have seen will end just like this.

4

The Moreton's hall was a big barn.
Through petalled glass windows of blue and brown,
I watched the family bring in the hay.

A timber lisped. A mullion
Creaked its sermon of Progress.
Whispers of linen drift between texts.

Newly astonished, paint under plaster :
Susannah repulses the elders' swift eyes,
Hoping to truss her delicate swathe.

Further, the gallery's blind Fortuna
Faces the harridan Destiny.
Lifting us up, light's wavering grains

Go on beyond us, curving to touch,
And warming. Motes of harvester's gold
Dazzle fat fish. Cattle just watch.

IX   *The failing pattern*

5

In dream I served as a Russian soldier,
Carrying morphine − expelled from his squad,
Sent with a nurse who changed to my mother,
(She who had heard of my territories),
Speeding across the wide Ukraine.
The blood−veined eye of narrowing war
Glazed as a shell exploded a church
With such concussion it shuddered our train.
We shared our fear's enshadowing,
Passing in silence to beaches and nets,
Mile on mile of self−containment;
Endless, at last, the black−massing pines
Entering sleep, the mountains, oblivion.

7

A Yorkshire Carol

A few unseeded strands of straw
Litter the varnished Nativity floor,
Plastercast donkey, father,
Mary and her diminishing doll.

Sun casts light, municipal walls
Have seen worse days − the courts are 'in'.
What once was wonder now is sold,
Along with hymns from junior school.

'She loves you, Yeah, Yeah, Yeah,'
Confided the radio, new in its gleam,
'What do you want if you don't want money ?'
I ask it in gestures, images, sums.

8

Wild Cattle at Chillingham

The cattle graze —
              on equitable depth
Of grass or heather burnt for grass.
Last or first inhabitants
Grooming the forest
                    they strengthen off.

Survival, yes —
              persistence
Is what the wind and sun appraise,
And I inhabit no difference —
Closing the Winter, moving from ice,
Clinging to seeds
              of withering patience,

Leaving a pattern
                    only in this :
Extinctions or insistencies
Sear us, storming our every defence,
Stiffen, daze,
              or bruise us with fruit.

9

'Who looks through the sea at me ?'
(Or as I asked before),
That pounding tabula rasa,
                    its curling sumps and razorshells ?

From Dorset to Northumberland,
We watched them burn their crop,
Windblown isles of reiving wheat,
Slumping sodden char.

NOTE

At 30 years, Saturn returns to its natal position in an astrological chart. These poems were written at this focus, out of a hard winter in the North of England. They involve a search into the nature of Saturn, the deity, his trammelled evolution and unremitting temperament, which establishes him as a cipher for certain tensions in British history as well as in the convergence of planetary influence with personal history.

Many echoes attend and inform these poems – among the voices half–heard here are those of Chaucer, the writer of the 14th Century Shepherd's plays, Andrew Marvell, Purcell's 'Dido and Aeneas', Mother Shipton, Hobbes, Simone Weill, the designer of the gable–painting in the Long Gallery at Little Moreton Hall, Cheshire (echoing, in his own way, the maxims of Robert Recorde, mathematician), the Beatles, Adam Faith and an imaginary author of a tourist guide to land adjoining the A1 motorway in North Yorkshire. Goya provided the stimulus for the vision of Giant Saturn in Section VI of the first sequence featured here.

The drawings are not illustrations; they hinge on specific lines and develop in parallel to the poems. The threat implicit in Saturn's discipline becomes physical and creaturely, and the denials and the transformations demanded by Saturn are fixed at their moment.

Poetry by David Annwn

Shadings (West Yorkshire Press, 1982)
Foster the Ghost (Bran's Head, 1984)

Prose by David Annwn

Inhabited Voices: Myth and History in the Poetry of Geoffrey Hill, Seamus Heaney and George Mackay Brown (Bran's Head, 1984)

Prints by Peterjon Skelt

One Harvest
News From the Fruit Farm
Bill Sykes: Oranges and Lemons
The Boy Who Cried Wolf
The Sound of the Longboats

David Annwn was born in 1953 of Anglo-Welsh parents in Cheshire. Since then he has lived in Staffordshire, Lancashire, Avon and, for nearly a decade, in and around Aberystwyth in Mid-Wales. His poems have been published widely and he reviews regularly for **LABRYS** and **ANGLO WELSH REVIEW**. He teaches in Wakefield, West Yorkshire, and lives in a small house overlooking the M1 motorway.

Peterjon Skelt was born in 1955 in Ickenham, Middlesex, and grew up in Somerset. He studied at U.C.W. Aberystwyth and at King's College, London, where he researched the work of Lee Harwood. His drawings have been published in various magazines and he has had a one-man exhibition at Bridgwater Arts Centre, Somerset.